Breaking the Chains of Mediocrity

Breaking the Chains of Mediocrity

CAROL ROBINSON'S COLLECTED WORKS

Marianist *Articles*

CAROL JACKSON ROBINSON

AROUCA
PRESS

Originally published in 1947–1948
Used with permission

ISBN 978-1-9991827-6-2

Arouca Press
PO Box 55003
Bridgeport PO
Waterloo, ON N2J3G0
Canada
www.aroucapress.com
Send inquiries to info@aroucapress.com

Book design and cover by
Michael Schrauzer

CONTENTS

INTRODUCTION

THE ARTICLES IN THIS LITTLE BOOK, *Breaking the Chains of Mediocrity*, will discomfort the complacent Catholic. Though written seventy years ago, their urgent call has not lost any relevance: the Catholic life does not consist in a mechanical, mediocre practice of the Faith—one that simply meets the minimum requirements of being a Catholic in "good standing"—but in a fully-realized Catholicism that penetrates into every facet of one's existence. Unabashedly Catholic, the ideas formulated in this work may well challenge the reader to confront his own spiritual mediocrity.

Carol Jackson Robinson (1911–2002), wrote these five articles for the *Marianist* magazine at the beginning of her literary career, while she was as yet unmarried, and just several years after her conversion in 1941. Although she was still wrestling with how to view the world through a Catholic lens, she was at the same time co-editor, with Edward Willock, of the intrepid Catholic periodical, *Integrity* (Volume 1 of which is available from Arouca Press). In the early issues of *Integrity*, she wrote under her pseudonym Peter Michaels, which she also used for the *Marianist* articles; her reasons for doing so are unknown, but perhaps she hoped that masculine identity would ensure that her ideas were taken seriously, especially given their controversial nature.

Carol Robinson majored in philosophy at Wellesley College and Indiana University where she developed an analytical mind. She wrote, in a retrospective article for *The Wanderer*, that she studied Descartes, Berkeley, Hume,

Spinoza, Kant, Hegel, Dewey, Plato, and Whitehead, but with scarcely any attention to Aristotle—and never in the pursuit of what was true.[1] For Robinson, as she explains years later in the pages of *The Wanderer*, the intellect naturally seeks what is true, and can, by the use of reason, come to a knowledge of the existence of God. Modern philosophy, however, casts doubt on all these concepts. Her mind was unsettled by this and, like so many students in the face of the skepticism of her professors, she lost what little belief she had in God, as she was raised by an atheist father and a liberal Protestant mother who was a lapsed Catholic. She began to take what she called "the low road to despair," but was rescued "just in time by a grace of conversion to Catholicism,"[2] having been brought to the Faith by a Catholic Action lecturer, Paul McGuire, and Dominican, Fr. Francis Wendell. It was these two who inspired her to begin *Integrity*. Fr. Wendell was the director of the Third Order Dominicans in the United States, which Carol Robinson would later join.

Shaken by her experience of despair, Carol Robinson began to set down her observations on a world she saw as slipping away from Christ and into spiritual mediocrity. She minces no words when she describes this as a calamity. Too many Catholics, she says, were turning away from the demanding life to which they were called by the sacrament of Baptism and were taking the easy path of compromise with the World. Their faith was having no effect on their actions in society and was at best a privatized affair left for church on Sundays.

1 Carol J. Robinson, "A Summit Meeting of the Two Cities," *The Wanderer,* (St. Paul, MN), September 11, 1986.

2 Ibid.

> ... Catholics ... are the most disappointing people I ever met. They are just pious unbelievers, that's all. They don't really believe a word of their own doctrine. Yeah, I know they say they believe it, but actions speak louder than words.
>
> Too many Catholics are wearing the Faith like a comfortable shoe instead of a sparkling new diamond.... Religion is something they do in their spare time, instead of the pivot on which their lives revolve.

While the Catholic Church was experiencing great material growth after World War II, Robinson was scandalized to observe that American Catholics exercised little influence on their society, that they were not becoming leaven in the world. In short, they were bound by the chains of their mediocrity, inert and ineffectual.

Meanwhile, the agents of secular mediocrity—marketeers, media pundits, professional sports players, Hollywood celebrities, etc., etc.—were spreading their worldly ideas unfettered, and radically altering the face of society. If only Catholics were as zealous. Sadly, seventy years later little has changed and the situation is worse than ever. Mediocrity breeds indifference and indifference leads to a loss of faith, as is witnessed by the great falling away from the Faith in the United States.[3]

In these dire circumstances, is Robinson being foolish when she exhorts mediocre Catholics to break free from their chains? Certainly, she knows how difficult the attempt can be:

3 While there are many factors that can be attributed to this decline, the statistics gathered here from 1970 to 2018 are quite telling: https://cara.georgetown.edu/frequently-requested-church-statistics/

> There is no way out of mediocrity which does not involve a conversion from worldliness to other-worldliness. One must cultivate precisely those habits which we tend to overlook, precisely those habits which will make us unpopular, singular, conspicuous, and all those other things which we so long to avoid.

Robinson was convinced that Catholics must reform existing corrupt systems which have proliferated while the faithful have languished in their self-imposed shackles. In this she was a radical (from the Latin, *radix* = root) for she wished to get to the root of the problem. She asks, "Who is stopping us from making the world Christ's?" The answer is only too obvious. The laity are in a position to transform the world—if only they would become Christ-like.

Becoming Christ-like is not easy, of course, especially when one's spiritual muscles have atrophied through inaction and easy-living. The Catholic laity must make a firm choice and not be swayed by worldly thinking. "We have got to be incorruptible if we are to do Christ's work. We must literally flee from adulation and honors and especially from riches." Perhaps unsurprisingly, Robinson wrote in advocacy of the Catholic Land Movement, promoted in many circles during the 1940s as an alternative to the way people lived in urbanized centers. City life made it all too easy to become attached to Mammon, and that can lead only to spiritual mediocrity. Yet Robinson does not advocate an idyllic retreat from society either; that would likely foster an individualistic pursuit of sanctity. The world at large *needs* Christ, and only Christians, unencumbered by self-love and material concerns, can bring Him to it.

Robinson's diagnoses and prescriptions were conditioned

by her time and place, but they remain valid for us today, because human nature and our conditions are fundamentally similar. Indeed, when Robinson writes of "perfecting men and their talents rather than deadening the human thing in the interests of mechanical monsters," can we not say today, having witnessed the brutalizing effects of systems that do not allow for this perfection, that her words were prescient?

This book touches upon only a fraction of the ideas Robinson explored throughout her nearly fifty years of writing, much of which has only been rediscovered recently. We hope that with this book, the first volume in our *Collected Works* series, Carol Robinson should be ranked among the most perceptive of 20TH-century American Catholic essayists. Her insights have remained in obscurity far too long.

CHAPTER 1

Pious Unbelievers

MARCH 1947

I'M NOT A CATHOLIC, SEE. I DON'T believe anything very much. The way it looks to me life is a kick in the pants. Your heart aches for there to be meaning, and there is no meaning. You fall in love. You are in seventh heaven, and it fizzles. The girl who makes your heart sing for months, whose very presence can transform a dirty subway station, well, what happens to her? One day you suddenly see that she is just a mediocre person, on the dull side. Worse still, you are mediocre too. That's the trouble, this mediocrity. A man ought to be noble. Don't ask me why. I figured it out once that the Greeks were right about their ideas of tragedy. A man ought to be noble so that when he dies it's more than just too bad. Not that he goes anywhere when he dies, or gets any reward, but just for its own sake. Maybe I believe that virtue is its own reward, I who hardly know what virtue is. Anyhow, the alternative to nobility is unthinkable. What if a man died without having lived intensely; having always played cautious, hugged money, never gone out in the rain without rubbers; what if he was nobody when he died and nobody cared? When I think of how horrible that would be I want to fling my life away for a great cause. I want to leave my job and travel as a common sailor to the ends of the earth in search of … of what? I want to stand on top of a country hill looking down on billowing fields of grain. I want to fling my arms wide to embrace the sun and the air and the clouds. Did you ever try to find a country hill like that? Well, don't look within a hundred-mile radius of New York. All my fine dreams usually end anti-climatically with my resigning the stupid job to which I am chained at the moment, to march forth colorlessly for one half day's celebrating in Central Park. A week later I am ignominiously scanning the want ads over a meat pie at the Automat.

Well, what I wanted to say about the Catholics is that they are the most disappointing people I ever met. They are just pious unbelievers, that's all. They don't really believe a word of their own doctrine. Yeah, I know they say they believe it, but actions speak louder than words.

Take the matter of money. It says as plain as anything in the Bible that it is better to be poor than it is to be rich. Sure it does. How about "Blessed are the poor," and that stuff about the camel and the needle's eye. How about "Blessed is the man . . . that hath not gone after gold, nor put his trust in money." Now most of the Catholics I've met are poor, but far from rejoicing in their state, I don't think it an exaggeration to say that taken all in all they are falling all over themselves to acquire the goods of this world. I've worked in offices with dozens of Catholic girls. You know the type. They are all alike. They wouldn't be seen dead with the same dress on two days in succession, and they are always sending out for sandwiches and coffee from Schrafft's. It has to be Schrafft's. It can't be Liggett's. They eat twice as expensive dinners as I do, and they'd change their jobs at the drop of a hat for more money. I worked in a bank once where a stenographer's husband committed the *faux pas* of the season. You know what the dreadful thing was that he did? He called for his wife dressed in his working clothes.

She was disgraced, I'll tell you. You know what kind of work he did? He was a carpenter. Doesn't that strike you as pretty peculiar, that a Catholic should be ashamed to admit her husband was a *carpenter*?

I'm really concerned about this poverty business, because in my more lucid moments it seems to me that the Bible is right. The kind of mind I've got, I have to figure everything out. So I say to myself, "Maybe it *is* God speaking in the Bible, and if it is He ought to know what He is talking about. Let's have a look around and see if there is something good about being poor that there isn't about being wealthy." Well, I could see right off that the poor don't have to worry about burglars making off with their jewelry cases or about Amalgamated Tire's being off three-quarters of a point in Wednesday's closing. But after I thought awhile I could see some more subtle advantages.

It seems to me that poverty is the gateway to freedom. We've got it all mixed up. We think that a guy who just inherited a couple of million can do what he pleases. Maybe, but I doubt it. Anyhow, the people who aren't rich and who want to become rich are just plain slaves. Did you ever figure out the cost, I mean the spiritual cost, of getting wealthy these days? I have, because there's a lot of pressure put on me one way and another to become a respectable success.

Now the way I see it, to get ahead in the world you always have to be an opportunist. There's a way to get rich in every age and all you have to do is to get on the bandwagon. Back a couple of hundred years you did it by owning land. Then it was by building up the railroads and other utilities. Then it was heavy industry. Then insurance companies and newspapers and department stores. Then it was advertising. Then radio, and airlines, and public relations. Notice that the means get less honorable as you go along. It's a far cry from George Washington, landed gentleman, to Pegee Fitzgerald and her commercials-studded breakfast table.

The way to make your millions right now is black marketing. Now it is a curious thing, but all the Catholic lads I know are feverishly going to commercial night schools in order to get into advertising. What's wrong with them? Advertising is finished as a gold mine, for one thing. If you want to make a million dollars that's not the place to do it. I tell you, to be a worldly success, if that is your ignoble aim, you've got to be an opportunist. By the time any kind of business has been reduced to neat little principles, put into textbooks, and is taught in night schools, you can be pretty sure the big boys of tomorrow have moved on to riper fields.

But apart from their miscalculations, why would anyone want to go into advertising? Can't they read? *Haven't they heard of The Hucksters?* Don't they know that almost every advertising man in Westchester County has been ill at ease with himself since he first got into the racket and has been drunk several times a week since to hide from himself his own lack of self-respect? Why should they aspire to carry on the inglorious tradition?

But that's not the full answer to the poverty question. It must be better in itself to be poor than to be rich. At least that's the way I tried to figure it out. I finally decided that the advantage lies in having a better view of reality. I have a rich aunt who hasn't any idea of what the score is. I mean she lives in a sort of "let them eat cake" kind of world, in a positive cloud of unreality. She leads a gay social life, with every one including herself pretending to be what they aren't. They pretend to be happy, only they are not happy, so they have to have a few drinks to create the illusion whenever they meet. They pretend to be pals with people they don't even know or care about. Her husband, he's a banker, prides himself on being friendly with his lesser employees, but my goodness, he hasn't even dreamt what goes on in their heads. Same way with my aunt. She has the most curious and erroneous notions about the character and cerebral activity of her colored cook (who's a fine woman, poor in reality and in spirit) and the bank employees, among whom I worked incognito, as it were. Well all these poor, or more or less poor, people have a nodding acquaintance with reality. And as for my aunt and uncle, they certainly have their number. They understand my honored relatives as though they looked at them through X-ray machines.

Do you see what I'm driving at? Between the classes there is not a mutual understanding, but there is a one-way understanding, and it's on the part of the poor. Of course my investigations are not conclusive, but tentatively I am entertaining the hypothesis that poverty gives you an "in" with reality. And the advantage of that? I don't know. I only know it's terribly important. You've got to keep hold of reality. Maybe then you will find the truth some day.

Anyhow, I myself am trying to achieve freedom through poverty. If a man would live simply, without pretensions, he would be practically free. The way things are now you have to kill yourself and your ideals to keep up a stupid standard of superficial living. I'd like hardly to have to work at all for awhile till I get things figured out. Did you ever read Thoreau? He had some good ideas and I figured the Catholics would too.

What difference does it make whether the Catholics do or don't? Lots. The trouble with me is that I'm no Thoreau. I talk big but I can't be heroic in a vacuum. I've got to have a point to life, an ideal, and a community and a whole lot of things. By myself, and uncertain, I'm nothing. One day I quit a job because I'd rather starve than pretend the work is significant. Then I get hungry and go job hunting again.

I met a Catholic once who was the most different person I ever saw. That's really what keeps me searching among his co-religionists. Met him on a bus going out to Chicago and he gave me his address but I lost it. Worst mistake I ever made. This Catholic was married and about thirty. We got talking about economic security and birth control. His theory was that God is not bound by a rotten economic system and that if you did what was right and just you'd turn up with enough meals a day to keep going, and anything else that was really necessary. He kept quoting "Seek ye first the kingdom of heaven and all these things will be added unto you." He claimed it really meant something and that he'd tested it out. For instance, he had five kids and his economic position had all along been what you might call precarious. This was just after the depression, and he and his family had been through it without missing a meal and with a few extras at Christmas time. His jobs hadn't been ideal, but not bad either. He had quit twice in protest against injustices to other people; so you couldn't say he had compromised his principles. He considered the matter of having children as they came sort of a test of faith, and he laid it down as a general rule that God will supply extra food for every extra child.

I was tremendously impressed by him, especially since he had tried it and it worked. Since then I've had a morbid interest in the size of Catholic families. Margaret, my sister who is a social worker, claims Catholics fight to get birth control information. I don't know about that, but the fiver year old daughter of Mrs. Monahan in our office let it out at the Christmas party that she was going to have a little sister as soon as they could find a bigger apartment. My pal on the bus would have reversed the statement: that the bigger apartment would be forthcoming, somehow, upon the new arrival.

Now you understand what I mean when I say Catholics are pious unbelievers. I keep watching them. I see that they have never heard of the lilies of the field. They fall over themselves to get insurance for this and insurance for that. They take out annuities at 16. Notice how they monopolize the civil service "security" jobs. I've seen a bride force her husband out of chemistry, which he loved, and onto the police force. I've seen Catholics play safe in everything from not joining unions in the formative stage to refusing to join first Friday clubs for fear they wouldn't get ahead in the office, to marrying men just because they were good providers.

And why don't I get married at all? Well, I'm looking for something, and I haven't given up yet. Love? Maybe. Some kind of love anyhow. But not sentimentality. I hate sentimentality. I hate the sentimentality of social workers. I detest the softness of counselors of college students who tell you not to work too hard. I hate to hear mothers forbid their children to play rough games. What do they think life is, a tea party? I abhor the unctuousness of Protestant ministers. I could never listen to Alexander Wollcott and his tear-jerking tales about stray dogs. There's something wrong somewhere. We've gone on a maudlin emotional jag. But I think there is, or was, something clean and hard and real and noble called love.

That young man on the bus was still in love with his wife, more so, in a domestic life characterized by clothes lines of drying diapers. I was telling him about the love I mean. It is something that completely transcends this common-place life that you and I are enduring. I found myself using rather extravagant words, like ecstacy and rapture, because I couldn't think of any others. Don't laugh. Is it my fault that the French movies have cheapened their meaning? You know what the young man told me? He said the words had been borrowed from Mystical Theology (that has something to do with the saints) for analogous use to describe the heights of human love. He said religion was a love affair between man and God that culminated in utterly blissful experiences. He said a lot more things I couldn't remember afterwards, but they thrilled me at the time.

Afterwards I sounded out every Catholic I met for six months but I didn't find a single one who had ever heard of the contemplation he talked about. I was going to go to a priest, but I kind of lost heart.

So that's why I'm drifting around. That's why I consider life just a kick in the pants. I want to give myself, and the world urges me to sell myself. I want to lose my life, but the Catholics aren't sure that I should risk it to find my life. I want to sell everything to purchase a pearl which ought to be selling for a great price, but which is lying tarnished on a bargain counter.

I wish I could meet that young man again. I wonder if he is still a Catholic. Maybe it was he, not the Church, that got me. If it was the Catholic Church it is certainly carrying around a lot of dead weight in the form of pious unbelievers!

CHAPTER 2

How to Convert Catholics

JUNE 1947

IT IS HARDER TO CONVERT CATHOLICS than it is to convert other people, but it is very rewarding. As a Catholic Action lecturer once said to me: "Don't worry about the Protestants; if we could only get the Catholics to be Catholic, the Protestants would fall over themselves in their haste to join the Church."

I have myself observed the truth of his statement. People are not attracted to the Catholic Church on the basis of average virtue. They do not reckon: "Let's see, taken as an average, ninety per cent of the Catholics I have met have practiced forty per cent more virtue than the Lutherans and eighty percent less adultery than the Unitarians; so I guess I'll join the Catholic Church." No, that's like figuring that if there were 10,000 missionaries in China, and if each converted 100 Chinese per year, etc. The truth is, of course, that the job could conceivably be done by one St. Francis Xavier, and might very well fail of accomplishment with 100,000 missionaries.

A man may meet in his life several thousand "unconverted" Catholics. Let them be virtuous, respectable church-going people; yet our man may never feel drawn to Christ's Mystical Body. On the other hand a man's Catholic encounters may include several first-class heels, along with sundry drunks and murderers. But let him just once meet a man who has allowed Christ's life to transform him, just once see someone in whom God is fleetingly rejected, and his pulse will quicken, his steps will turn in the direction of the Source of that Life. Leon Bloy, in the intensity of his inner life and the miserable conditions of his material life, was such a magnet. The beauty of the Faith penetrated his writings, which were otherwise and literarily no great masterpieces. This was so much so that the impoverished Frenchman could cry out that "there is only one unhappiness, not to be one of the saints." Jacques Maritain was one of the those who heard his echo of Christ and drew near.

Let us get back to the matter of converting Catholics. The reason it is hard to convert them is that they are suffering under the illusion that they are already Catholic. What then is lacking? From what must they be converted? Well, chiefly from mediocrity and unbelief.

MEDIOCRITY: DIAGNOSIS

As aforesaid, quality not quantity is the measure of the Church's strength. The same Catholic Action leader told me: "It would be better for the apostolate if we had fewer Catholics in the United States and they were better ones. We are weighted down by mediocrity, which throws a smoke screen in front of the faith."

Too many Catholics are wearing the Faith like a comfortable old shoe instead of a sparkling new diamond. They have watered it down to external activities, instead of to a change of heart. They recite perfunctory prayers and sing sentimental hymns, instead of crying out to God from the depth of their being. Religion is something they do in their spare time, instead of the pivot on which their lives revolve.

In the Apocalypse St. John writes: "And to the angel [bishop] of the church at Laodicea write: Thus says the Amen, the faithful and true witness, who is the beginning of the creation of God: I know thy works; thou art neither cold nor hot. But because thou art lukewarm, and neither cold nor hot, I am about to vomit thee out of my mouth. . . ." What does that mean? It means what we don't like to believe, that God may prefer the Bowery bum, perpetually drunk, to the respected citizen and the complacent Catholic Committee woman; and the reason is that the former at least bears testimony to God by his anguish at being separated from God, while the latter fails to catch fire in the very presence of the flame. Holiness does not consist in self-righteousness (this was the pharisees' error and has characterized Protestantism in practice. That is the reason for the widespread revolt against religion today in our post-Protestant country. Let no one say that the contagion has not spread to, and diseased, many a Catholic).

Holiness especially does not consist in negative righteousness (I never blaspheme, never look at women – "thank God, I am not like other men, sinners"). It does not even consist in our own virtue. Holiness is the supernatural life, is God's life, surging through us and pervading us. Our role is to allow it to do so. We get the Life from the Sacraments, and the only predisposing condition on our part is humility. So the drunk in the gutter, who cannot help but know his own utter failure, is in a way terribly near to God. Natural despair is very close to supernatural hope, because it is when we know we are nothing that we are ready to admit that God is everything and to cast ourselves on His mercy. This is the key truth discovered by Alcoholics Anonymous. They do not go to fellow alcoholics when they are on the wagon, but when they are in Bellevue alcoholic ward, just having failed utterly for the nth time. They do not say, "Pull yourself together, man," but they do say, "See how persistently and utterly you fail by yourself. Cast yourself upon the mercy of God."

Look at it another way. Christ said that He is the living water, and that if a man drinks of Him he shall no longer thirst. This is the secret that the saints have discovered and the source of their peace. But many a man who is thirsting for the Living Water, not knowing where to find Him, tries to slake his thirst with the firewater of whisky, and finds it unquenchable.

The mediocre on the other hand are those who have neither drunk deeply, nor do they thirst. They are those who sip Coca-Cola and wonder when the new automobiles will be generally available.

Mediocrity hangs over America like a pall. That is why Monsignor Sheen can say that God may be more pleased with the Russian people than with us. There is an intensity, a spiritual intensity, deeply imbedded in the Russian temperament. It is hard to imagine any considerable number of Russians falling for an ideal of "comfort." Asceticism, suffering, intense joy, profound melancholy, wild gaity, are all part of the Russian nature. They incline to hate God or to throw away everything for the love of Him. They are either hot or cold.

MEDIOCRITY: PRESCRIPTION

The essence of mediocrity is that we cling to our lives instead of dying to ourselves that God may live in us. In the case of Catholics it is not usually because they have not received grace in the Sacraments, because many mediocre Catholics are even daily communicants; the difficulty is that they have not died to themselves.

Granted that it is hard to die to yourself in an age which encourages feverish activity and endless concern with what we shall wear and how we shall decorate our houses, and which pyramids committee meetings on top of committee meetings. Nevertheless it must be done. The first step away from mediocrity is to realize that it takes heroism to be a Christian today.

There is no way out of mediocrity which does not involve a conversion from worldliness to other-worldliness. One must cultivate precisely those habits which we tend to overlook, precisely those habits which will make us unpopular, singular, conspicuous, and all those other things which we so long to avoid. It will not always be tough going because in the end we will have maneuvered ourselves into another set, another way of life, far better than the original one. But we might as well face the fact that the beginnings will be difficult.

The essence of the new program will be penance, mortification, intensification of the Sacramental life, development of the interior life, prayer. Start going to Mass instead of to novenas. Turn off the radio and see if you can endure the silence. Drop out of the mad race to be well dressed. Start giving alms at the sacrifice of luncheon desserts. Observe strictly the fasts prescribed by the Church. Try to pray without a book or a rosary. Do spiritual reading. Cut down on the movies. All these things will be the first beginnings of the road which leads to sanctity. You will need a spiritual director to help you along.

Now it is an odd thing about Catholics that it is precisely this *conversion* they resist with all their might. They will go to more and more meetings, give more and more money, talk more and more; but please do not ask them to about-face. If they did, they would cease to be mediocre.

A conversion means a turning *away* from something, and a turning to something else. The first conversion (the spiritual life is a series of them) means a turning away *from* the world and a turning to God. Most converts from outside to the Catholic Church are strikingly aware of this and are quite prepared for their lives to be transformed. They have entered into a new economy, the economy of salvation, and everything they do from there on is a step toward God. Mediocre Catholics are the people who won't come in or go out. They shy away from mortal sin, but they won't turn all the way toward God. That's why they don't progress in holiness. They mark time, but they can't mark time forever. "In our time it is impossible for anyone to be mediocre," said Pius XI. And so it is. These mediocre Catholics are under an ever-increasing strain. Presently they will fall either all the way in or all the way out of the Church.

UNBELIEF

"Yeah, but you've *got* to earn a living!" This is the theme song of the unbelieving Catholic. The thing he chiefly doesn't believe in is the Providence of God. If you say to him: "But seek *first* the kingdom of God and His justice, *and all these things shall be given you besides*," he will answer you, in effect, by saying that you have to be practical. Practical means you have to seek first the kingdom of mammon, lest you starve to death, and that is to say that you just don't believe what Christ says. Some people may not think that it is very important not to believe just some certain things in the Gospel, but as a matter of fact the whole goes together. Either you believe the Church or you don't; there are no intermediary stages (although there is a lot of procrastination, ignorance, and vacillation). The people who don't believe that the just man lives by faith will be found upon investigation to be somewhat incredulous about dogmas beginning "Credo in unum Deum. . . ."

In my own experience this is more and more borne out. The other night I was discussing her business with a greeting card saleswoman, of Irish descent and convent education. She was trying to explain why you can't have a religious theme on your Christmas cards because that will make them unsuitable for the Jewish trade, and I was telling her, somewhat irritably, that her position just didn't make any Catholic sense. Later on in the evening it came out that she was, as she put it, "tormented by the Devil with doubts." What she meant was that she had as good as lost her Faith.

There are thousands and thousands of Catholics in the same spot. They still go to church, usually. They still know the Catholic lingo, although they have a distaste for discussing spiritual things. They are still held by the thin thread of sentiment to a Church in which they no longer believe.

Now, we live in a world of middle thinking, but out of it all there comes a certain secular creed, having dogmas like these: "God is unimportant." "*This* world is the one we have to make into a paradise." "Science is omniscient." "Money is all-important." "Psychiatrists (not priests) know all about the soul." "You can't live without sex." Etc. Etc. It comes in over the radio. It's knee-deep in all the mass-circulation magazines. It utterly pervades secular education (I know a major public college in which, as far as investigation can tell, not one single *truthful* proposition is taught). It is hawked in the movies. It is common gossip. It is the basis of all business. It is so bad that it is almost true to say that "either what the Church says is true, and therefore everything the world says is wrong, or vice versa, the world is right and the Church out of its mind."

The sad situation of Catholics is this: they want to believe the Church, but they eat up everything the world says and, in effect, order their lives accordingly. How can they do both? They do it by a combination of ignorance and sentimentality. You never catch them reading a Catholic book of theology, even if they are studying secular philosophy. They go in for novenas, partly with the "gimme" spirit, but partly too for the *emotional* satisfaction they get out of it. Emotion does not carry over into daily. Out of this situation arises the curious and sad phenomenon you very often see in the Church: a pious mother (as measured by devotions) who opposes every effort of her daughter to go into Catholic Action, while pressing her to become a worldly and financial success.

The advantage of coming into the Church from the outside is that you already know, when you become a Catholic, the secret that is still hidden to the Catholics: *the utter bankruptcy of the non-Catholic world.* We are in a world which is dying of despair, while Catholics (hastily throwing the pearl of great price under the kitchen stove) sit around and admire it. They think (having been themselves poor for so long) that the rich build country estates and go about on yachts in a delirium of joy. They do not. They keep erecting palaces, making music, laying out gardens, and changing dresses to hide from themselves their internal disquiet, the aching of their own hearts. The emptiness of their godless lives. The last place that they who so need help will look for hope, is among those who keep copying and admiring their own futile efforts.

The pagans keep writing stuff that they themselves do not believe, saying things that have a tinny ring even in their own ears. How we betray them when we believe it! There are thousands of examples. One interesting one is found in psychoanalysis. There are plenty of Catholics ready to find this pseudo-science "very interesting," and containing a number of truths. While we sit by and admire (kicking off into a corner the sword of the spirit which is the word of God and which happens to be lying around), someone like Clare Boothe Luce slashes through its error like a knife. Does the Freudian say we all secretly desire to return to our mother's womb? All that means, says Mrs. Luce, is that plenty of us wish we had never been born. Has St. Augustine said: "Thou hast made us for Thyself, O Lord. . . ."? It is Mrs. Luce who has just fished it up from the dust-heap in the corner and is lost in the joy of knowing it.

The remedy for unbelief is Faith, and Faith is a gift. Don't be too proud to believe something you haven't thought up and examined for yourself. Take God's word for it. Don't think that everything God says has to be examined in the light of opposing errors. Faith increases, and becomes more and more luminous, and makes us sing out that what the Church teaches is true, in proportion to how much we cherish and *believe* it. Cut out the national weeklies and the national monthlies. Abstain from the radio. Skip the tabloids. Subscribe to a Catholic library.

Where was it that you dropped that sword? It ought to be lying around here some place; let's shine it up and gird ourselves with it.

CHAPTER 3
We Can Do All Things
SEPTEMBER 1947

Dear Fellow Catholics:

THE WORLD IS HOLDING ITS BREATH in the hope that we will rescue it in this moment that remains before it plunges to its final destruction. This is the lull before the storm, the opportunity before the end of all opportunities, the great moment to which we alone can rise.

Why us? Aren't we a sorry lot to be the hope of the world? Yes, we are. We're weighted down with mediocrity, bespattered with worldliness, filled with vices, petty and great; to most appearances one with a weary, wasted world. No, hope is not in us because *we* are anything, but because Christ is in us, however well hidden, and Christ can save the world, even at this eleventh hour, through us if we will let Him. "I can do all things in Him Who strengtheneth me," said St. Paul. Paul, you will remember, was a little nobody, practically alone, without wealth or letters of introduction, who undertook to Christianize a considerable part of the Mediterranean region. It was a little as though your cousin, Mary Jane, were to undertake to save Russia. "I can do *all* things in *Him*," said St. Paul. The corollary to that is found in Our Lord's words. "Without me you can do nothing."

Shall we consent to save the world? Or shall we stand aside and have a last movie and coke before we collapse with the world? The decision must be made *now*.

OUR IMAGINARY ENEMIES

It just happens that at the moment all the doors are open for us to walk into them. That is not true in Europe, where people are old in their sin and too hungry to arouse themselves to another crusade. That is why the Holy Father, and millions of others look to America.

Who is stopping us from making the world Christ's? I spoke to a group of social workers not long ago, with very interesting results. Instead of treating of some minute problem of social work in the technical language of the profession, or engaging in safe generalizations, I plunged into the heart of the matter and questioned the why and wherefore of the very foundations of social work. Afterwards, one after another of the audience came up to say, "We've been waiting twenty years to hear that," and "Thank you for daring to come out in the open," and "That's just what I've always secretly thought." It was gratifying to hear this at first, but then I became curious. My admirers were of all shapes, sizes and positions. Of whom were they afraid that they hadn't spoken earlier themselves? I finally concluded that they had been deferring all these years to a purely non-existent enemy of honesty and frank speaking.

Similarly, it is commonly thought that the priests and bishops of the Catholic Church will automatically be against any effort on the part of the Laity seriously to practice their faith. "You'll never get away with that," is frequently heard. But I have seen a dozen or so "daring" precedents ventured without so much as a raised eyebrow by way of reaction, and I have even heard of a diocesan chancellor who privately said that he wished the laity would do something on their own initiative for a change.

There are no laws in the Church against Catholic lawyers

reforming the legal profession, doctors studying theology, real estate men trying a Christian solution to the housing problem. There are not even prohibitions against undertakers praying for the dead or secretaries changing to dish-washing jobs or carpenters founding St. Joseph societies to build houses for the poor. We act as though we thought the hierarchy would be complacent as long as we as politicians used bribery, as publishers published heresy and pornography, as ordinary citizens orientated our lives to avarice, but that they might frown upon us if we went so far as to practice our Faith in our daily lives. Isn't it about time we realized that the clergy might have Christ's interests at heart as much as we, possibly more, and that they will not faint with horror at the appearance of help from us?

But the avenues aren't open to us to make over things. Aren't they? They have never been so open. Find the publisher who is not receptive to a good Catholic book. What makes you think a group of girls or men with a new plan couldn't take over a wing of the state insane asylum? Wheaties might not sponsor your radio program, but if it is any good you can get it on the air free through the courtesy of the station. It's a simple matter to get a permit for street speaking, and what's more, people are ready to listen with friendly curiosity. Is the city too big to raise kids in? Move to the country. You can't? Of course you can. Ten thousand organized Jocists could by their collective might in Christ move Detroit out into the Utah desert and build Christian villages every five miles from Dayton to Columbus, if they wanted to. We are the only people with real vitality in the western hemisphere. Will we bestir ourselves and take over for Christ, or shall we turn over for another session of day-dreaming?

OUR REAL ENEMY

Our only real enemy, besides ourselves, is the Devil. He is to be cast out with prayer and fasting, which will be the cornerstone of all our activity. We have strong reinforcement here from an ever increasing army of contemplatives.

If you know the Devil's tricks you can laugh at him. Now his tricks today are these: to set all the problems in other than Christian terms. He has capital and labor fighting so hard that you won't notice that that isn't the real economic issue. He camouflages the spiritual discontent of teachers and nurses so that even they think it's a matter of money that's spoiling their appetite and giving them that listless feeling. He has wives thinking a new refrigerator or a delay between babies will have the salutary effect on domesticity that only something like family prayers can really accomplish. Laugh at the Devil and feel free to examine society's diseases in your own perspective.

IT'S SO EASY

Anyone can take over the world who wants to. It won't always be that way. Now it is. You can see an analogy in the political field. There are no obvious presidential candidates because of the low caliber of the generality of politicians. We are about to witness a contest between midgets. Now if there were one man of integrity, one man concerned with the common good, who had a well-thought out plan for effecting it, he would be hailed with boundless enthusiasm. He would be elected by popular acclaim even if he weren't championed by either major party. Yet there is no one, because no one has dared to follow the clean path of civic duty instead of the befouled trail of organized politics.

Honesty, intelligence, simplicity, goodness—just these qualities alone, without genius or family or pull, would serve to set a man in the lead. And what if a man is holy? With light from the Holy Ghost, and Charity and courage, and prudence, how welcome such a man would be wherever there is real work to be done!

Another point. It is easier today to lead a completely Christian life in disregard of established custom, than it is to try to be a Catholic and worldly success (or even on inconspicuous worldly conformist) simultaneously. What is hard is to lead a double life, to try to please God and Mammon, and it gets harder every day.

OUR HANDS MUST BE CLEAN AND EMPTY

"Every man has his price," says the world cynically. And it is almost literally true. The world says it so bitterly. What it means is "We looked to you to be better than us, to be incorruptible, and you are no better than we. So we shall return to our cups to assuage our despair. We would have followed you anywhere if we had not been able to buy you."

When the books are balanced on the last day, it will be seen that the Catholics of 1947 who should have been making over the world couldn't, because it would have meant less money, and the loss of security. The threads that bind us to the world instead of Christ are made of nylon.

Every man has his price. With some the price is a little higher. They are the Catholic actionists who start out generously and then make a good thing of it like the sociologists who start to make a better society by setting up a coordinating committee with themselves as members, at a comfortable annual fee, or the social workers who start establishing justice by giving themselves a month's vacation.

Now it happens that the apostolate offers opportunities for self-glorification. You can become a big-shot there even if you are of no consequence in civil life, and you often get about with richer and more cultured people than theretofore. Nothing is more pernicious than the "prominent Catholic layman" mentality when it really sets in.

We have *got* to be incorruptible if we are to do Christ's work. We must literally flee from adulation and honors, and especially from riches. An almost invariable sign of health in the lay apostolate is the spirit of voluntary poverty, and it is frequently found, thank God. We must choose a frugal life and make it quite clear to ourselves that that is where we belong and are going to stay. Then when the manager offers us a sudden raise of $10 a week (which we know in our hearts is a bribe to keep quiet about injustice among the other employees), when the local politician comes to us with a good proposition, when the local movie theatre sends us free tickets and the black market offers to cut us in, we will have already gathered our strength to resist.

At a certain company which pays the highest salaries in the world, men sell their souls at an average of $75 a week, with extras (which include everything from college courses to sanataria) thrown in. All you have to do in return is to worship the company and its president, work at high speed, and suppress the criticism of means and ends which rises in your throat. "I will give you all this," said the Devil to Christ on the top of the mountain, "if only you will worship me."

As voluntary poverty offers a measure of protection against material bribery, so must Catholics arm themselves against the much more insidious temptation to fame, the appeal to their pride and vanity. This can only be done by constant intensification of the life of prayer. We must look to God and not to the world for our satisfaction. If we do so, and if we act more and more in accordance with the will of God, the world will end by hating us, and we will have escaped the death-dealing lure of flattery.

THE TEST

There is one simple way of telling whether you are doing God's work or just messing around in another worldly plan. If your scheme will work without holy people, it's of the world, not God. It is too late now for any *natural* plan to work, any plan which does not involve the change of men's hearts. All our problems now are really spiritual problems.

It is on this point that the world and Christ are diverging with great rapidity. Everything that is "of the world" is becoming more and more highly mechanized and systematized. Men, where needed at all, are incidental, and replaceable. But the things that really *need* doing will depend on people of caliber and sanctity. You can't build good marriages without good husbands and wives. You can't make a society without a community and that involves people living together in harmony, an almost impossible task now. You can't have good schools without good teachers, teachers who have a greatness of their own and are not just organs of a method. You can't convert America without Catholics in whom the joy of the Faith overflows.

WHERE TO START

It is well to start in an obvious place, with a real problem that badly needs solving. To start at all presupposes a group of Catholics with some spiritual development, unity, and great earnestness. I shall presuppose, for the purpose of these articles, that such already exist. What then?

In one sense it is impossible to say what to do, because the Holy Ghost will guide us, and each one must find his own vocation. But on the other hand it is rather simple to point directions, because there is nothing mysterious about what needs to be done. There are certain fields of action, all of them practically untouched as yet by Catholic effort, which must be entered. For instance, there is the whole field of spreading the truth, there is the problem of restoring people to mental health, the necessity of breaking down swollen cities, the need of a new intellectual synthesis, and the remodeling of the economic order. I shall sketch some of these problems and their possible solution in future articles.

CHAPTER 4

The Breakdown of the Cities

NOVEMBER 1947

THE REASON THAT WE HAVE TO BREAK the cities down is quite simple. It is this: Our present cities are antithetical to Christian living, militate against even natural life and virtue, and indeed threaten life itself (both in the long run because city people do not reproduce themselves, and in the shorter eventuality of atomic warfare). There is no alternative to the breakdown of the cities. There are no good arguments for continued superconcentration save those personal considerations of the shortsighted real estate speculator and politician.

OUR CITIES ARE CANCEROUS

The problem is complicated by the fact that a normal city is really better than the country because it allows for the greater development of men's several gifts. Similarly, it is normal and good for body cells to increase as we grow to adulthood. But it is not good for cell-growth to run wild as in cancer. Just such a cancerous chain of growth has produced our abnormal cities, which not only fail to satisfy the elementary functions of social man, but also threaten to exterminate him. Or again, our cities are like subway crushes. It is good for men to become members one of another, but that's an entirely different thing from being stacked together in an underground car.

Our cities are the physical manifestation of a way of life consonant only with an all-pervading commercialism. The alpha and omega of their existence is profit. We have big factories instead of little factories because the owner can get richer that way. We want people to stay in the metropolis to keep up real estate values. Farm hands take jobs in factories because they are paid more. Small shop owners sell out to chain stores because there's money in it. Wives keep jobs instead of having children because it affords them more luxuries. The urban masses are scarcely less touched by avarice than the capitalists. The modern American city is the house that love of money built. Its symbol is the skyscraper. Like the church, the skyscraper is a functional building. Of what possible use would it be for anything other than business?

THE ORGANIC AND THE MECHANICAL

Things that are done God's way reach, usually slowly, a just size, and then stay more or less the same. Cancerous growths can't stop. Our cities have long since outgrown any sort of just size. There is nothing economic about them. Take the telephone system, for instance. It is cheaper per unit to have two telephones in a city than only one; cheaper to have two hundred than one hundred, and so on, but there comes a time when further increase in the number of telephones does not reduce the cost per phone but increases it. This has long been true in New York City, for instance, where the rates keep going up with the number of telephones. The same thing is true of the traffic problem. Each new device for controlling traffic is relatively more expensive. Or again, the whole process can be seen in merchandizing. At first the large department stores, octopus like, absorbed all the little stores, in the interests of profit and the name of efficiency, so that women within a fifty mile radius of New York were all forced to shop in a dozen or so emporia. Now that the competition has been obliterated, the large stores are starting branches in the suburbs, little replicas of the big store. Do the branch stores have the same variety of goods as the large stores? There is no variety in the big stores any more. The process of centralization has been paralleled by a process of standardization. And of course there is also this notable difference, that whereas there were formerly many shop owners there is now only one store owner and his thousands of minions. The situation is inimical to individual ownership and responsibility. It is also inefficient.

You can see the same thing in housing, where the true nature of centralization reveals itself very clearly. Is it pure chance that housing projects so strongly resemble prisons? Or is it because they are, in a sense, prisons, and we the voluntary inmates?

Yet in a sense it is not true to say that our mechanized life goes against our nature, that is to say our present nature. We have perfected machines and systems instead of men. It takes a tremendous amount of spiritual formation for men to live together in peace and harmony, and reciprocally to serve each other. Mechanized life is a substitute for the flow of virtue among men. When men are formed Christians they can get along with each other in the intimacy of a family or a community, with a functional interdependence. When they are not themselves perfected, it is necessary to isolate them by systems and conventions which conduce toward toleration and impersonality. The only duty which a fellow subway passenger has toward you is to bathe with Lifebuoy every day, because your only relationship with him is that of physical proximity.

The way we live in modern cities is awful and inhuman, but perhaps it is the only way in which dehumanized and spiritually underdeveloped people can tolerate each other.

RUSTIC RUIN

We must be quite clear about this: the problem is not simply to choose between an evil city and an idyllic country. The choice is between an intolerable urban condition and a very badly diseased country. Both the rural and the city diseases come from an orientation to Mammon. The country is commercialized too.

The rural distortion is basic. It shows in the fundamental pattern of our country life. The pioneers were already rugged individualists rather than members one of another in Christ. Whereas in Europe people had traditionally settled in little villages with farm lands outlying, here in America men mostly staked out huge farms and built their houses in lonely isolation from one another. They were mostly religious men, but the church was no longer the center of their corporate lives and so there was no real basis for a community. The European tradition persisted, however, in New England where there remains beautiful architectural evidence of the simple Puritan communities in which a common life and culture did flourish, but could not endure because of the truncated nature of their religion.

From our wrong roots have developed today's ruins. The farmers have succumbed to commercialism. Their big, isolated farms are getting bigger and bigger, are being sold to large corporation holdings, and are worked with a minimum of men and a maximum of machinery. Even such small farmers as remain exploit the soil, follow the one-crop, get-rich-quick system and eat what they buy at the chain stores in town: condensed milk, butter substitutes, and white bread. The brightest sons always go to the city. The burden of work on a commercial farm, even with machinery, is crushing, and is as dull as a city clerk's job without being as clean. Farmers are men of business, with business ideals and bourgeois living habits. In many rural sections the moral degeneracy would shock an habituee of Times Square.

NOT A MATTER OF CHOICE

The reason then for leaving the cities is not to choose the good life which exists in the country in place of the bad life of the city; it is to choose the possibility of a good life, as against the inevitability of ruin. Not everyone will leave the city or the factory, but those who would lead us out of our slavery will have to provide for some sort of mass exodus, of which they must be the pioneers. It is enough of a case for decentralization that the temptation to the practice of birth control in the city is already overwhelming. The new housing allows no quarter for so large a family as God might send, nor does it seem likely that the family wage will set in short of state subsidy for cannon fodder. In the city a man cannot make new beginnings any more than he can build a house in Times Square, or pitch a tent on Wall Street. In the country there is a hard struggle, but it is with nature, over which God intended man to have control. Any long-term plan for the salvation of souls must lean heavily on the reorientation of population. It will have to start with new communities, not isolated family farms. Some of the new villages will grow naturally into towns and cities, but normal towns and cities. However, the beginnings will have to be small.

COMPROMISE SOLUTIONS

Beware of schemes for having your cake and eating it too. Everyone is ready to endorse plans for living in the city while enjoying the advantages of the country, or vice versa. These schemes try every combination. At one extreme is the big-city penthouse, which brings a few flowers and shrubs to the very top of skyscrapers, completing the city's resemblance to Babylon. Of course life in a penthouse is about as countrified in reality as a honeymoon on Broadway is like a honeymoon in Bermuda because the happy couple have their pictures taken against a nautical backdrop. But, anyhow, the very slight advantage of penthouse life over just ordinary apartment life is enjoyed by a mere handful of the rich.

At the other extreme is another handful of rich people who are enjoying urban life in a rustic setting. These have country estates with air conditioning, built-in bars, and yachts or limousines to deliver them to Radio City or the financial district. They are in the vicinity of nature, but not leading natural lives. Again, they too are the few.

In between are the vast hordes of suburbanites. Now the experiment in suburban living is a recent development. You might say that it is an attempt to combine city and country on a fifty-fifty basis. Has it worked? No. In general the suburbs have succeeded in combining the worst features of the city with the worst features of the country. The advantage of living in the country is that you can lead a more natural life, but there is nothing natural about the suburbs. There are no cows or chickens, just dogs; not fields, but lawns. Community life, such as it is, centers around the country club or the A & P. The suburbs are vast dormitories trying to be playgrounds.

INDUSTRIAL DECENTRALIZATION

Real communities grow up around the Church. The industrial decentralists want to start communities around little factories, the workers having patch gardens. This is another palliative which will not work. It has not worked for Henry Ford, or for the Government power projects, or anywhere else that I know of. The idealistic planners who expect people to have a vigorous common life around a supermarket, a movie theater, a dam, or an automobile-part factory, know nothing about human nature. Several thousand housewives who have nothing to do except listen to soap operas and buy finished products according to trade mark, can and do form a sea of loneliness and a nightmare of backbiting. It would be bliss to get back to the cozy community life of the slums, where the Church still penetrates and there are remnants of a cultural past.

A variation on industrial decentralization is "homesteading," in the colloquial modern sense, which means having one foot on the land and one in industry. It is a good compromise because (unlike most industrial decentralist schemes) it admits to being only a compromise. It means having a few productive acres on the edge of town or within driving distance of the factory or office. It is a half-way station for those on their way back to rural living, or a permanent stop for those too old or enmeshed to make a full break. The good thing about homesteading is that it doesn't picture the millennium in terms of industrialism. It just recognizes realistically that many who can't get free can still arrange to come up for breath now and again.

THE FRAMEWORK

The French have a saying about their government, that the more it changes the more it is the same thing. So it is with schemes for making life more tolerable within an industrial-capitalist economy, which is to say, an economy oriented to money-making. The life of a radio executive penthouse dweller is made of the same colorless stuff as that of the machine hand in the industrial garden city, and both are as remote as possible from the former life of the European peasant or squire. Catholic reform must shift to an agrarian-craft economy in which the small land owners (subsistence farmers) and craftsmen set the tone of our economy and society.

An agrarian-craft society is not the same thing as a return to the stone age to start all over again. There can even be some assembly lines left if anyone wants them, and heavy industries may well remain. It is a matter of balance, a matter of having (at least for most men) machines as tools rather than as masters. It is a matter of perfecting men and their talents rather than deadening the human thing in the interests of mechanical monsters.

THE FIRST STEP

Spiritual development is more important than any other single factor in the land movement. Underlying all the failures to date (Catholic and non-Catholic) has been this primary cause, that the people lacked spiritual discipline and, as a consequence, the ability to live together in community, and to sacrifice for an ideal. Not droughts and invasions of insects so much as quarrels and selfishness have seen the end of so many schemes that it seems as though the land movement is impossible to achieve. Yet in itself, moving communities of people into rural areas is not so very great an undertaking, not nearly so ambitious, materially speaking, as one of a thousand or so of our war projects. But in a war factory you could bribe people, at least temporarily, with high wages and fine washrooms, and what did it matter if they came out more degraded than they went in? In a land movement you can't disregard the human element. It is the hardest job in the world to make over men, but that's where you have to start.

The place to begin is in the city. It will take several years for a group to become congenial and spiritually formed in Christ, before it will be wise to make any beginnings. And the mere passage of time won't do it. There will have to be a framework for development, like Jocism, and a spiritual life sufficiently intense to dispel the false charms of urban life.

TECHNICAL TRAINING

Along with the spiritual training, those in the land movement will have to acquire a wealth of skills, whether in farming or crafts. Some may continue to teach or write or practice medicine, but there will have to be a farmer-craftsman basis. Here we can't help thinking that Catholic Action has the ideal framework for sponsoring a land movement. It would not be the main work of Catholic Action, of course, as that apostolate never rests except in the salvation of souls as an end. But if the Catholic Action movement were to decide to sponsor an exodus, it could provide the means in the services through which it operates, and among these services could be training centers for young men and women in the crafts pertaining to their future life.

It is more difficult to set up an agricultural school than a business school. Farming has to be learned by the apprentice method and is best taught on small, balanced farms, since that is the sort of farming desired. There are no such small farm schools now, but some of the state agricultural colleges are good in most respects. About ten years ago the Midlands Catholic Land Association of England made an experiment with training and settling unemployed city workers on the land. From the training point of view the experiment was very successful. On a larger farm than would have been ideal, and with an average of twenty men being trained at a time, with paid management, the cost over a period of three years was less than $3,000 a year, and there was a profit on the farming operations proper throughout. That particular project failed to materialize for tragic lack of money and sympathy, and considerable coldness on the part of the government. Msgr. Ligutti was having the same non-success in this country at the time because New York City preferred (for reasons that only a real estate man or a politician could fathom) to support men on the dole rather than have them gain independence on the land. However, the training part of the English program was a proved success, and showed that the cost involved is not so great as to stand in the way of such an organization as the Young Christian Workers when it gains its strength. It is also conceivable that someone would give the money, but at present the trend of thought of rich benefactors is indicated by the fact that one of the Catholic colleges is building a new $1,000,000 business school.

Craft training is also in a disordered state, owing to over-specialization. Few men in the building trades could build a whole house. One way or another the land movement would have to provide good training in simple construction and crafts. Their construction training would have to start from woods or stone quarries. The only way to get a house today is to build one, and preferably not from prefabricated materials.

With this warning—that the right sort of training, both for agriculture and the crafts (the same goes for domestic science) is not to be had for answering the school announcements in the advertising columns—we shall leave the matter of technical training. Working out this sort of problem is much easier for the American mentality than seeing problems as a whole in the light of the Faith.

THE LAND MOVEMENT IS AN APOSTOLATE

The ultimate goal of any Catholic Land Movement is the salvation of souls, whether one envisions the new beginnings of a holy America, or just wants desperately to escape the driving temptation to birth control. It is not a means of turning one's back on a dying society, or of despising one's brothers who are bound to the assembly line. A hermit monk does not seek a cave because he is indifferent to the souls of men, but because he loves God, Who accepts his penances and prayers as earning graces for others besides himself. So those who go on the land must not be tempted to form a closed, self-sufficient society where they will escape the disaster which threatens all others. This could easily be done, for the corporate strength of religious men is very great. The Mennonites and the Mormons of our own day and country illustrate how prosperous a community can become with a religious ideal and discipline. Despite the fact that these groups are in many respects most admirable, they do not represent the Catholic ideal. There comes a sterility in the midst of prosperity; they somehow fail to overflow and sweeten the life of the whole country, as did the monastic orders in Europe.

So some sort of connection must remain with the city. It may be a bridge maintained by the Young Christian Workers for the continued exodus of families into a more Christian air. Or it may be that the community's chief work will be correlated with the needs of their less fortunate city brethren. One can imagine also a land community growing food for the bread line in a city House of Hospitality (as in the Catholic Worker), or providing vacation or convalescent homes for city workers. Or the community could center around an apostolic printing press (as in Eric Gill's Ditchling in England), or music (as the Von Trapps) or sponsor a Christian curative center for the insane (as at Gheel in Belgium) or an art center, or even an apostolic movie company. If then, those who live there have their shoes handmade by the community craftsman, is that so terrible? In the cities only the very rich have handmade and well-made shoes. And if the people of the community dress as pleases them and becomingly in the sight of God, is that so awful? Remember there will be no girl at the next desk to jeer because you are not in fashion. But the transformation from shoddy commercialism to healthy simplicity will be gradual, though there will be compensations from the very first. No one will regret the passing of tawdry escapist pleasures, and as the movement grows it will set a new ideal of goodness before a pleasure-jaded and despairing society.

CHAPTER 5

Today's Battlefront

JANUARY 1948

THERE IS A LOT OF EXALTATION OF the Common Man these days. The Common Man is just an ordinary good guy, whose reading is limited to the comic strips but who has a heart of gold. One of the chief misfortunes of the contemporary world is that the Common Man does really exist, legions of him — brainless fellows ready to be herded around by any dictator who will use them. Newspaper feature writers like to pretend that today's battle is on the level of "meaning well." It isn't! The battle today is the battle of the intellectuals, and whether the world (and many souls) will be saved or not, will be settled in the realm of truth.

LEARNED IDIOTS

There are legions of so-called intellectuals who are as remote from the battlefront as are the common men. They are the learned idiots and the insincere men. They know a lot of facts, but not the ones that are staring them in the face. Many college professors are of this type, especially the decadent liberals. They talk and talk. They describe in detail the tribal customs of the Polynesians (without really understanding anything about them). They compare Shakespeare's mention of trees with Milton's mention of tress. They know all the whens and wheres and none of the wherefores and whys of history. They write learned papers on the effects of domestic cockroaches, on the metal hygiene of only children of suburban albinos. In a word, they are the sophists of the ages, the men that Socrates complained about, who are still very much with us. They play around with truths, but they have no regard for truth. Their books are masterpieces of self-contradiction and double talk. They are the spiritually blind teachers of the day. Their keynote is insincerity. They themselves do not believe the things they say in classrooms and on lecture platforms; that is, they do not believe them with their hearts and minds so that their whole lives are lived accordingly. You can see this very clearly in the anthropologists. They usually conclude their years of study of the working and playing habits of primitive tribes with some such generalization as that all men need to worship a higher being. But that does not bring them to their knees. Having prescribed for all mankind, they promptly make an exception of themselves.

CHRIST, CURIOSITY, AND COMMERCIALISM

There are two ways of approaching knowledge. The first, an honorable approach, is through a thirst for truth, which exists in all sincere men. They will not rest until they have understanding and wisdom. They are not at peace until they have their bearings in the universe.

Intellectual curiosity looks superficially like a search for truth. It means "seeking to know second and third and fourth things before you know first things." It is a sin, a sin against our intellectual nature, because it tries to go against the order of learning. We have to know first things first, just as certainly as we have to know our destination is Chicago, in order to set out on our journey. If you are only going to know incidental details instead of directions, you will be like children seated in the motor car of their parents or herded in the boxcars of a dictator, seeing trees flash by, on the way to an unknown destination. Curiosity is the inevitable result of secular education, which we shall take up in a minute.

The tired stage which succeeds curiosity is marked by intellectual indifference. Then men say, "Never mind what's true or what isn't true, let's get sick." We're in that stage now. It is a stage of dog eat dog, of competitive fortune-seekers trampling everywhere on beauty, truth, courtesy, privacy, dignity, and order. It means the complete disregard of the common good. Men will not stand for this anarchy, this chaos, indefinitely. It is almost finished.

SECULAR EDUCATION

Secular education is of its nature, and as it exists in this country, ultimately ruinous. It pretends to mean, let every man hold his own views about the important things such as the meaning of life and the existence of God and the nature of the soul. It progresses into teaching, by blatant implication, that there are no important truths. This is the present state and it is intolerable to man's nature (which thirsts for truth in spite of him). The public schools are now passing into the third stage, of a synthesis against God.

But there is another thing about secular education which always marks it. Someone has to run the schools and that someone is the state, which means the people who run the government. Now it happens that this power which governs the schools always has to be the best of all possible powers, at least in our democracy. As public officials do not look at God and beat their breasts, so the schools do not regard eternal principles and criticize their nation by comparison.

In the public schools *our country, our form of government, our ways* are the best, by a dogma commonly consented to. We are on the right side of all our wars. Our economic system is the best. Our virtues are the important virtues, our shortcomings are the least of all shortcomings. Tolerance and mixed religions are fine because we have tolerance and mixed religions.

The net result of all this is that the public school and state college students come out of school with a deep-set conviction that everything is *essentially* right in America. They only see accidental things wrong. They see that bathtubs and automobiles and college degrees are not universal enough. They never question that these are the important things.

But even this frame of mind is coming to an end. Certainty, and a higher cause to fight for, are demanded in the nature of things.

THE NEW SEARCH FOR TRUTH

We are now in the era of absolutes: absolute devotion, absolute truth, absolute dedication. We see here in the intellectual field a situation analogous to that in the economic field. It was never known before in history that economic profiteering was exalted and considered socially respectable. It will not be known tomorrow. Whether the Communist or the Catholics take over, it will again become a sin against the common good for a man to seek first his own gain.

Similarly in the intellectual field. Agnosticism and dilettantism are going out and we are about to enter the era of sincerity and conviction and high principles.

Before we discuss this welcome turn of affairs, it would be useful to point out that the liberal, indifferentist position is diseased and perverted now. It has curious manifestations, and none is so curious as the search to learn truth from error. You see this in shaky Catholics. One told me the other day that he was going to read the philosopher Kant. "Have you read St. Thomas Aquinas?" I asked. No, he hadn't. He hadn't even been through an advanced Catechism. But he had heard that Kant took exception to some of the Catholic ideas (which ideas he hadn't bothered to learn) and he thought he ought to have a broadminded look at the critics. He even admitted that no one believed Kant by way of first principles and so Kant must be wrong.

The secular version of this error is to try to ferret out at least descriptive truth from imperfect or distorted specimens. Take the psychologists, for instance. They try to learn all about men from studying children. They spy on children at play and derive learned principles from it all. When they are not doing that they are examining criminals, that is, bad men. Or they study insane men. Or they go to the Hottentots and examine primitive men. If they wanted to know all about starfish they would pick the best starfish they could find, not one with a leg off, or a baby starfish, or a dead starfish, or a freak starfish. If they did the same when studying man they might learn something. Let them examine an adult genius or, better still, a saint, and they might begin to come out with some of the right answers.

THE NEW SYNTHESIS

Well, the future belongs to those who have their bearings in life, and that means first of all intellectual bearings. Unless you can size up reality you cannot proceed under your own power. You will be enslaved by anyone who cares to enclose you, because you will be moved only by obedience to a superior force, or by your appetites.

There are two synthesis arising, a false one and a true one. They are opposite explanations, but they both do purport to explain, and do explain, first things.

THE FALSE SYNTHESIS

The false synthesis has everything wrong, but it's dogmatic about it. These are the dogmas: this is the only life; beatitude is material beatitude of some sort (an all-electric kitchen or a new sex freedom); there is no God; there is no free will; there is no spiritual soul; there are no objective moral obligations.

This is the synthesis to which Marx and Freud have contributed liberally. Marx and Freud really did explain, even though badly, and erroneously. Marx told what history meant and where we were going and what was virtuous and not virtuous within that pattern. Freud has given us self-knowledge. He's told us how we work and why. It's plausible. It does explain in a sort of way, but it's wrong. Its consequences are frightening, but it tells "why" to a world tormented by the absence of explanation.

THE TRUE SYNTHESIS

We, of course, must make the true synthesis, and we have to make it fast if men are to act on it to save the world. Unlike Marx and Freud, who went by a sort of intuition, we do not have to worry blindly. We have all the first principles and many of the second ones. We have only to synthesize these with modern times and our daily lives. We can start on clear ground and certain ground.

Take the matter of self-knowledge Freud can't hold a candle to St. John of the Cross or St. Thomas Aquinas. But we haven't even read St. Thomas or St. John of the Cross, much less tried to apply their principles to the healing of disintegrating human nature.

We've done a little better with history, thanks to Chesterton, Belloc, and Christopher Dawson. We really do know what history is about and we really can bring order out of chaos.

Right now the Catholic synthesis is fighting toward truth on the economic level, on one hand analyzing the complexities of modern economics to see things as they really are, on the other hand searching St. Thomas and others for the principles to apply.

But it's going on everywhere, this synthesis making. Catholic scholars are tripping up the cocksure anthropologists. We are on the offensive (or should be) with the Planned Parenthood Association. We're fighting out the church and state battle, coming to grips with Hollywood, and revising textbooks and strengthening schools. The results are not yet apparent, or even decided, but there are signs of intellectual strength and determination everywhere. You even see it among the Jocists, for it is not for scholars only. The line must be held all the way down.

It's an odd thing about a synthesis, a reintegration. When we men want to analyze something, want to tear it down or break it apart, the process comes natural to us. The opposite process doesn't. To see a relationship between things not yet related we need more than anything else, light in the mind. This light will come to us from the Holy Ghost. Insofar as we are holy, insofar as we pray, insofar as we are utterly sincere and humble in our search, God will grant us light to see the radiant truth which lies already in front of our noses. We must see ourselves not only as ignorant (for that we are of our own Catholic principles) but chiefly as blind, and pray for the light. Our reconstruction of the world awaits our synthesis of religion and life today.

Also available from
AROUCA PRESS

Meditations for Each Day
Antonio Cardinal Bacci (pbk & hb)

Fraternal Charity
Fr. Benoît Valuy, S.J.

The Epistle of Christ:
Short Sermons for the Sundays of the Year
on Texts from the Epistles
Fr. Michael Andrew Chapman

Our Lady, A Presentation for Beginners
Dom Hubert van Zeller, O.S.B.

A Centenary Meditation on
A Quest for "Purification" Gone Mad
Dr. John C. Rao

Integrity, Volume 1:
The First Year (October–December 1946)
Ed. Carol Jackson, Ed Willock

Christ Wants More: Ignatian Principles
and Ideals on Prayer and Action
Fr. Frank Holland, S.J.

AROUCA PRESS REPRINTS

Dogmatic Theology
Msgr. Van Noort
Volume 1: The True Religion
Volume 2: Christ's Church
Volume 3: The Sources of Revelation/Divine Faith

CPSIA information can be obtained
at www.ICGtesting.com
Printed in the USA
BVHW081332131221
623925BV00005B/64

9 781999 182762